Stop Smoking

A Concise And Effective Manual For Cessation Of
Smoking Without The Assistance Of Resolute
Determination

*(Cease All Tobacco Consumption And Remain Abstinent
From Nicotine)*

Christophe Spencer

TABLE OF CONTENT

A Closer Look At The Hitchhiker 1

Reconceptualize Your Mindset Regarding Smoking. 21

How To Stop Smoking Without Gaining Stress, Weight, Or Mood Swings 25

Potential Hazards Associated With Prescription Medications For Smoking Cessation 31

Confront And Overcome The Apprehension Towards Potential Alterations. 39

Is It Advisable To Obtain Medical Assistance? 56

Cigarettes And Stress 73

Quitting For Good 87

Conclusion 123

An Introduction To Your New Life Free From Tobacco Products 154

Establish A Clear Smoke-Related Goal 163

A Closer Look At The Hitchhiker

Oftentimes, the majority of individuals when traveling by vehicle encounter a hitchhiker on the roadside. In such instances, how do we typically respond? We refrain from offering any assistance. In fact, the majority of us feign ignorance towards the hitchhiker's presence. We simply proceed by driving without stopping. What actions must be taken to ensure we do not provide transportation to a hitchhiker?

I beg your pardon? Could you please rephrase or provide more context so that I could assist you better in finding an alternative way to say the same thing in a formal tone? Nothing! Nothing at all.

This constitutes positive news, which is commonly neglected due to its excessively intricate nature, concerning the cessation of smoking. Once more, for the umpteenth time: Engaging in smoking is an action performed by us! However, relinquishing smoking is not an activity that we undertake, but rather a cessation of it! (Do you recall this being conveyed previously?)

What procedural steps must one take to refrain from offering a ride to a hitchhiker? What precautionary measures need to be taken to avoid participating in a bungee jumping activity? To not rob banks? To abstain from registering for mud wrestling. There is no obligation for you to undertake any action. Simply take the opportunity to unwind and decompress. Be who you are. It is advised that you refrain from engaging in any activities that may pose a risk to your safety.

Furthermore, it is recommended that you continue with your other activities, but without partaking in smoking, bungee jumping, or mud-wrestling. Refrain from engaging in any actions or behaviors that deviate from your true nature and refrain from partaking in any activities that may be deemed unsafe or unsavory. Trust the natural course of events to unfold organically thereafter.

If you have been providing regular ride-sharing services to the hitchhiker, who is frequently smoking, for a considerable period of time, we tend to regard the situation as more complex than it appears at first glance. We have the tendency to move towards the side of the road, position ourselves adjacent to the passenger seat, lower the window and elucidate to the elderly hitchhiker, known as Mr. T. My friend, may I inquire as to why we have decided not to collect him today? We may express all of our grievances regarding his larcenous conduct, extravagant tendencies, and the point of diminishing returns.

Mr. T. apologized by stating "okay, okay, sorry." I understand your complaints. Please refrain from worrying about arranging transportation for me. Don't worry about me. At present, it is not necessary for you to rendezvous with me. Not at all. I'll just wait. Please proceed with your other endeavors. I shall remain in this position until further notice. No problem. Sorry. (Mr. T. He exhibits a tendency to make statements with a view to ingratiating himself with you, regardless of their veracity, since he may be deemed a prevaricator.

You proceed to depart, yet you are unable to resist the urge. You observe him through the rear view mirror. He is present with a contented expression, affirmatively acknowledging your actions while attentively observing you. He perceives that you are observing him with interest. He waves. Muscle memory kicks in. You wave back.

We possess a comprehensive understanding of the events that are to unfold henceforth. You may continue with your affairs; however, at a later time, whether that be in the afternoon, evening, or following morning, you acquiesce. Ever since you departed, your mind has been consistently preoccupied with the unpleasant, unwise, and unpredictable hitchhiker. Eventually, you return to the location where he was positioned, the very spot where you had initially departed from his presence.

Yep. He's still right there. Kindly proceed to pull over to the side of the road and come to a complete stop. He greets you with a friendly gesture, a smile on his face, and proceeds to sprint towards your vehicle, whereupon he kindly unlocks the door and enters with a light, agile bounce. At least on his part, everything is instantly absolved. You two drive off again. He reclines comfortably in the seat allocated for the passengers. It is entirely at your discretion to allocate your personal resources in terms of possession, fuel, time and monetary compensation. He has resumed his position in the desired location. He retrieves the pack from his shirt pocket. "Excuse me, may I enquire if you would like to partake in smoking?" he inquires politely, with a smile, extending an offer of a cigarette. It is already within his knowledge that the sole purpose of your return was to retrieve him.

We have all experienced circumstances that have been somewhat disconcerting, exceedingly vexing, and surreptitiously embarrassing. It appears that we are unable to give up accommodating the hitchhiker, Mr. T. Uggh.

Instead of attempting to flee, let us pivot and scrutinize him more deeply to apprehend his methodology. Undoubtedly, a weakness must exist within him, which can be tactfully employed in our favor for gaining superiority and disposing of him eventually.

In order to gain a more comprehensive understanding of his character, let us pose a series of relevant questions and endeavor to provide corresponding answers. May I inquire as to the place of birth of the aforementioned hitchhiker? What was his upbringing like? May I inquire about his preferences in terms of cuisine? What fuels him? What's his story? What's his hold? What benefits is he receiving from our organization? Providing responses to these queries, however concise, is likely to confer an edge, possibly alleviate his hold, enabling us to depart.

May I inquire about his place of birth, please? To a certain extent, it could be posited that he came into being as a vulnerable infant at the moment of our initial smoking session. At that juncture, he lacked the requisite influence over us. We could lift and lower him. We were obliged to transport him manually. And yet...

We have not simply fabricated his existence. We did not embark on the process of air-drying and curing the leaves of an unfamiliar and exotic flora independently, followed by rolling them tightly and igniting them in order to assess the potential pleasure that may be derived from inhaling the resulting smoke. We weren't that clever.

No. Mr. T. It had been roaming the Earth long before our birth. He was present at this location, anticipating our arrival. It was not mere happenstance that we happened to come across him. The comprehensive historical account of how tobacco corporations purposely and strategically targeted children through their marketing endeavors warrants a separate publication. But Mr. T. He had been present on the planetary surface prior to his employment with the prominent tobacco corporations.

To illustrate, precisely seventy-two hours subsequent to his arrival, Christopher Columbus documented in his chronicle that they encountered an individual traversing in a canoe from the vicinity of Santa Maria unto Fernandia. Accompanying him were some desiccated plant materials which held great worth in their culture, evidenced by a voluminous portion of such materials that was presented to me at San Salvador. The indigenous population had been engaged in the farming of tobacco for countless generations, potentially spanning several millennia. Renderings of Mayan Monarchs depict a few amongst their ranks partaking in tobacco consumption.

Despite our parents and grandparents abstaining from smoking, we were nonetheless born into a society with an entrenched and advanced smoking culture. Since the earliest days of our observation, we had witnessed adults, including well-known personalities whom we held in high regard, indulging in smoking as if it were an innate and commonplace act. From times immemorial, pervasive promotional materials, explicit and implicit, have enticed us towards smoking by projecting its image as an attribute of style, desirability and daringness, even when we were illiterate. Despite the fact that smokers often perceive their habit as a private and individualized relationship with Mr. T, it is pertinent to acknowledge that he is an unapologetic adulterer who incessantly seeks novelty and excitement. Throughout the entirety of his life, even prior to our acquaintance, he has exhibited this behavioral pattern. He conveys to us that we hold an exclusive place in his heart, and when in his presence, the experience feels notably personal and intimate. He disseminates consistent falsehoods to all recipients.

Additionally, we have discovered that our departure and withholding of physical affection from him does not significantly affect him. Indeed, he never fulfilled his commitment. Another individual may shortly present themselves as a naïve target. Since we did not originate Mr. T., the hitchhiker, it is unnecessary for us to expunge him from existence. We have chosen not to engage with him any longer and have ceased participating in his frivolous conduct.

Therefore, the subsequent inquiry arises as to how he came to develop and occupy such a significant presence within our individual sphere. What substances does the individual consume for sustenance and inhale for respiration? What fuels him? Each of these inquiries can be responded to succinctly with one term: attention. Mr. T. The individual in question persists as a powerful presence in our lives by virtue of the level of attention we accord him, sustaining his existence, growth, mobility, communication, expression, and endurance. Attention embodies a transformative energy. The focus of our attention is instrumental in promoting growth.

Mr. T., the individual who is soliciting a ride, pertains to resembling the behavior of a stalker commonly witnessed in Hollywood movies. As the recipient of his attention, one may assume that any favorable attention conferred upon him would be met with immense admiration. It would be greatly appreciated if you, the prominent movie star, extended an invitation by stating, "Please do come in and join me by the pool, as my staff shall provide us with beverages," to Mr. T. would not argue. He would flash a smile, confidently enter the premises and linger until the arrival of the hearse.

Frequently, nevertheless, the individual engaged in stalking exhibits a detrimental association with the celebrity. Pardon me, but I find your presence discomforting. I kindly request that you vacate the premises. I advise you to refrain from any further attempts to contact me. Should you persist, I will be compelled to involve the appropriate authorities and pursue legal action, potentially including a restraining order. Furthermore, I have taken measures to ensure my personal safety and will not hesitate to utilize them if necessary.

Interestingly, the individual who is stalking takes pleasure in observing such occurrences. Upon receiving a verbal reprimand from the star, the stalker apprehends the fact that he holds a place in the star's life and is acknowledged by her. Despite the negative nature of their interaction, the stalker perceives a connection with the star and considers it a relationship. The crux of the matter lies in this: the individual in question (Mr. T.) evinces an indifference towards the nature of the attention he receives, whether positive or negative; any form of attention satiates his appetite. His sustenance and respiration are derived from the attentive focus given to him.

What implications does this hold for smoking habits in our day-to-day lives? Could you kindly describe the appearance of the object/person/place in question?

It is apparent that spending time near the swimming pool while indulging in beverages is a likely pastime. We consistently bestow our focus on Mr. T, extending invitations, allocating time, and accommodating him in all our activities from daybreak until bedtime. We commence our efforts by affording him a modicum of attention at the outset of the day, promptly followed by disbursing morsels of our attention intermittently throughout the day until just prior to retiring for the night, at which point we grant him a final salutary 'good night' attention. Several individuals even awaken during the nocturnal hours to impart further doting care upon him. This represents a customary mode of operation for many individuals who engage in smoking.

Conversely, we also file restraining orders against him. We express our aversion towards him. We consciously remind ourselves of refraining from smoking and abstaining from the consumption of tobacco products, resisting the inclination to indulge in Mr. T. ...either in this location, that location, or another location. We discuss him amongst ourselves and with others. We convey to our acquaintances and loved ones about his unpleasant demeanor- or they communicate such instances to us. We allocated considerable adverse focus on him, presuming that by providing ample negative attention, he would depart. However, he consistently fails to do so. He loves our attention. His sustenance hinges on the degree of attention we bestow upon him, irrespective of whether it is of a favorable or unfavorable nature.

Furthermore, it is not imperative to undertake any measures regarding the aforementioned observations at this stage. We're just studying Mr.T., seeing how he lives, how he ticks. A fundamental strategy employed in guerrilla warfare is to gain comprehensive knowledge about the adversary by closely monitoring their activities, identifying their geographical movements, and analyzing their routine practices. This constitutes the purpose of our presence here. Please be apprised that the individual in question, namely Mr. T, as evidenced by the observations presented, has become apparent. lives on attention. Yet another strategy employed in guerrilla warfare is to disrupt or sever the supply routes utilized by the adversary. It is with this approach that we shall proceed. Prior to proceeding, it was imperative to ascertain the source from which he obtains his fuel.

It has been ascertained that Mr. T's past is relatively extensive, as it has come to light that he had been present in this location prior to our arrival and had merely been impersonating a juvenile. We are cognizant of the source from where he draws his energy - it originates from the constant attention we accord him on a daily basis. However, we remain with a few unresolved inquiries. What is the nature of his influence over us? Alternatively, we may personalize the matter at hand. What influence does he exert over me? What is the reason for me consistently directing my attention towards him? Do I genuinely desire only his collection of nicotine, or does he offer something more valuable to me? Which narratives does he consistently share with me that I haply subscribe to and accept as true? I am diverting my focus towards obtaining something from Mr. T. What is it? What am I getting?

To provide a response to the aforementioned inquiries, it will be required of us to once again circumnavigate the block in this transport vehicle. Please consider Mr. T in a renewed perspective. Moreover, his ornate attire and choreographed dance movements. Please take a moment to reflect on the underlying reasons for your continued return to him. Naturally, an additional chapter will be required for this purpose.

Reconceptualize Your Mindset Regarding Smoking.

The act of altering one's perspective has the potential to transform and enhance the quality of one's existence.

According to research findings, a significant number of individuals who have successfully ceased smoking did so through an impulsive decision rather than premeditation. Research indicates that by experiencing varying degrees of motivational tension associated with smoking cessation, coupled with different environmental triggers, individuals can achieve a mindset shift that promotes an extensive and holistic transformation upon immediate abstinence from tobacco, as opposed to adhering to a predetermined cessation timeline in the foreseeable future. Essentially, smoking cessation is contingent upon one's mindset and attitude, rather than adherence to a specific plan.

Individuals who seek information regarding the expected course of the complete recovery process from addiction to nicotine are more likely to achieve success. Reprogramming your thought process plays a crucial and indispensable role in enabling you to successfully conquer your battle against smoking. Which attributes contribute towards the process of mental reprogramming?

Education

Undoubtedly, education is an immensely empowering tool. This augmentation has the potential to increase the value of education twofold with regards to smoking cessation. In order to attain permanent liberation from your nicotine dependency, the initial measure towards reconfiguring your psyche is to alter the signification of tobacco for you. It is imperative that you alter your association with the habit of smoking. It is pertinent to note that education can significantly aid individuals in this regard. Ensure that you acquire knowledge regarding the potential ramifications of nicotine withdrawal. Consume all available information pertaining to addiction, including its physiologic impact on the body and techniques for post-smoking cessation recovery.

Support

The immense worth of interacting with individuals who have either undergone or are presently undergoing the same circumstance as you, and possess the precise skills to motivate you, is truly invaluable. Currently, there exist numerous associations and societies comprised of compassionate individuals who can serve as role models in your endeavor to achieve smoking cessation. One may consider enrolling in these groups and forums to acquire valuable insights that can aid in the restructuring of their mentality towards smoking.

How To Stop Smoking Without Gaining Stress, Weight, Or Mood Swings

The experience of nicotine withdrawal, which is commonly despised by smokers, is an arduous repercussion consistently encountered during the initial weeks and months of tobacco cessation. The most challenging stage in the process of quitting smoking is frequently the one that causes individuals to revert to smoking. Typical indications include an increase in body weight, fluctuations in mood, and elevated stress levels attributed to nicotine deprivation within the system.

The experience of stress commonly arises during the process of withdrawal when individuals endeavor to cease smoking; they may encounter feelings of frustration and despondency caused by the absence of nicotine, which exacerbates their cravings. Individuals who rely on smoking may experience an increased level of stress due to a perceived absence in their daily routine. In order to preempt any potential encroachment of the quitting phase by said issue, presented below are a set of recommendations:

- Take care of yourself. It is imperative to maintain adequate hydration and follow a well-balanced diet in order to effectively preserve one's physical form and attain positive emotional well-being. It is strongly advised to incorporate the consumption of multivitamins into your daily regimen.

Please refrain from excessive consumption of coffee. The impact of caffeine frequently manifests as anxiety, a condition that can significantly exacerbate the stress levels experienced by smokers during their cessation process. It also engenders challenges in the realm of sleep, exacerbating the extant stress and other symptoms of withdrawal that are currently being endured.

Unwind and destress with a rejuvenating massage and a soothing bath. Both of these are highly effective stress-reducing techniques for individuals of all backgrounds. The physical manifestations of stress-related tension across the body can be effectively alleviated.

- Sleep right. A substantial proportion of individuals who quit smoking tend to experience fatigue during the initial weeks of abstinence. Hence, sufficient amount of sleep plays a vital role in diminishing the level of stress experienced by individuals.

- Stop being so serious. Individuals who have decided to quit smoking should not excessively stress themselves about achieving a flawless quitting journey. This has the potential to exacerbate stress levels and potentially lead to additional setbacks. It involves the dual process of directing concentration towards a task while simultaneously easing one's mind and body.

The acquisition of weight occurs during the cessation phase due to the fact that nicotine consumption, which burns approximately 200 calories per day for heavy smokers, naturally suppresses the appetite. Larger appetites experienced during the cessation of smoking are attributable to the physiological effects of abrupt nicotine restriction on the body. Presented herein are some guidelines for achieving a desired physique whilst concurrently quitting the habit of smoking:

- Exercise, exercise, exercise. The decelerated metabolism caused by the abrupt cessation of nicotine necessitates increased physical exertion. Engaging in daily physical exercises, including structured workouts and brisk walking, can prove efficacious in achieving the intended outcome.

- Eating right. A sound physique is inherently the result of a harmonious blend of physical exercise and dietary habits. It is strongly recommended to consume fruits and vegetables on a daily basis. It is advisable to refrain from consuming high-calorie foods, particularly sweets, to the maximum extent feasible during the withdrawal period.

- No drinking of alcohol! Alcohol tends to have high contents of calories. Moreover, this alluring libation serves as a catalyst for smokers to succumb to their detrimental vice, as the consumption of alcohol and smoking of cigarettes are known to be mutually reinforcing.

Lastly, the withdrawal phase is characterized by the challenging symptom of mood swings, which pose a significant challenge to manage. The manifestation of abrupt heightened feelings of rage, tedium, and desolation can pose a significant challenge to those seeking expedient resolution. These frequently result in a state of depression that necessitates the use of specific medications as a means of recovery. The singular and exclusive means to effortlessly overcome fluctuations in mood is by consistently maintaining a positive mindset. Positive thinking serves as a complementary factor to positive emotional states.

Potential Hazards Associated With Prescription Medications For Smoking Cessation

The utilization of prescription medications is prevalent amongst individuals endeavoring to overcome their smoking addiction. As the population of individuals attempting to quit smoking continues to increase, additional pharmaceutical interventions are being researched and produced to guarantee successful cessation. Presently, the prevailing options in the market include Chantix and Zyban. The benefits associated with these pharmaceutical products are accompanied by their own set of drawbacks. Adversely consequential outcomes are frequently observed in relation to these synthetically-produced commodities composed of diverse hazardous compounds.

Chantix is the foremost product for aiding in smoking cessation due to its absence of nicotine and generally innocuous consumption. Among various drugs, it has been observed that it provides the greatest degree of pleasure akin to that which was previously attributed to nicotine. In addition to its efficacy, this product is also highly utilitarian and reasonably priced. What are the potential drawbacks or adverse effects associated with the use of this medication? Chantix may present adverse effects, including but not limited to headaches, nausea, and insomnia. It has the potential to elevate the likelihood of particular cardiovascular and respiratory ailments.

Zyban, conversely, is among the most recent and encouraging pharmaceutical options for smoking cessation available in the market. It functions as an antidepressant, subsequently mitigating the incidence of cravings. It elicits a comparable impact on the brain and Central Nervous System resembling the sensation of gratification observed with Chantix. The adverse repercussions of the therapeutic medication comprise of cephalalgia, xerostomia, tussis, pruritus, and abdominal discomfort. Zyban has been prohibited in several nations due to its toxic nature, which has the potential to result in significant health complications.

On the fourth day, it is recommended to take the initial step of becoming a member of a community dedicated to eliminating tobacco use.

It is imperative to acknowledge that undertaking the entirety of the task on your own is not feasible. You need help. Assistance must be provided by individuals who have previously confronted and surpassed the challenges you are presently experiencing.

Should I lack the knowledge of how to execute running, I would be inadequate in instructing others on the same. Thus, the same holds true for this particular instance. Seeking support from seasoned individuals can be highly beneficial in your quest to quit smoking. As such, I recommend enrolling in an anti-smoking community to avail yourself of their guidance.

On the fourth day, it is imperative to adhere to the second step with unwavering commitment, which entails remaining dedicated to the community.

Merely being a member of the community cannot guarantee your salvation. It is imperative that you demonstrate a strong dedication to the tasks that they may assign to you.

You will be solicited to participate in activities, thus it is recommended that you be prepared to adhere. This will alleviate the burden of contemplating on how to spend your leisure time during this cessation phase.

Your sole obligation is to adhere to any directives you may be given.

Day 5

On the fifth day, as per the initial step, what changes occur in the event of refraining from smoking? Prepare your mind.

As smoking constitutes an addiction, cessation of its use may elicit unpleasant physical symptoms that manifest as deceptive indications.

It may potentially induce melancholy, despondency, debilitation, or even dyspnea. It is imperative that you are equipped and ready to handle any challenges that may arise.

Failure to do so may result in a relapse of your smoking habit.

When such events occur, typically one may experience a sensation of impending demise, yet this sensation is fallacious.

It merely presents an illusion that might entice you to reinitiate smoking. It is imperative that you make adequate preparations for it. It cannot be escaped. It will surely happen. However, in the event of its occurrence, with adequate preparation, one can successfully surmount it.

Confront And Overcome The Apprehension Towards Potential Alterations.

Numerous individuals possess awareness of being on an erroneous trajectory, yet exhibit reluctance towards rectification and personal growth, a circumstance that frequently materializes. The issue lies in the correlation between the amount of time one invests in negative and harmful habits and the consequent escalation of retribution in the long run. It is akin to traversing along the precipice of a cliff, being cautious not to falter.

Thus, the optimal moment to initiate a transformation is presently.

You need to take the bull by the horns and pay the price all at once. We stand to reap substantial benefits and avoid a considerable amount of hardship, discomfort, discontentment, and exasperation.

Numerous individuals tend to opt for inaction over confronting a challenge and identifying optimal courses of action. They may perceive a sense of loss or decline, resist the relinquishment of possessions or attachments, harbor an ambivalent attitude towards change, or simply be apprehensive about personal growth and development.

Indeed, one is constantly undergoing transformations and progressions that occur ceaselessly, minute by minute, second by second, albeit unbeknownst to oneself. Your actions will elicit consequences commensurate with them. Despite a lack of conscious cognizance, it remains indisputable that noteworthy events occur within our lives on a daily basis, yielding concrete outcomes.

Should we acknowledge our inherent human condition, which entails possessing a unique identity while retaining the capacity to alter our values and behavioral patterns, we shall endeavor to forge a fresh path. In doing so, we shall have the agency to determine the individual we aspire to become and the mode of living we wish to adopt.

I will disclose to you a confidential piece of information...

Enhancing something implies a pronounced elevation of its quality, augmenting its intrinsic worth and thereby acquiring a significant progression. This can be likened to discovering a rare gem amidst a trove. Hence, relinquish any reservations and employ your entire potential to opt for those things that will invariably augment the worthiness of your life. Ultimately, opt to achieve it in its entirety to enhance the quality of your existence, and to attain complete personal and human fulfillment.

Upon having triumphed over your apprehension and realizing that progress is being made rather than sacrificed, the next course of action is to acquire the proficiency to surmount the hindrances within oneself...

CHAPTER NINE

Tobacco Discontinuation Instruments for the Practitioner of Family Medicine

Ask and Act

The USPHS endorses the application of the five A's in a concise intervention for patients who engage in smoking. The AAFP promotes and empowers its members and their medical teams to inquire about tobacco usage, and subsequently take steps to offer assistance to patients in quitting. The Ask and Act program, implemented by AAFP, employs a systematically developed approach grounded in USPHS recommendations for tobacco cessation. This remarkable and uncomplicated approach provides an opportunity for every member of an educational cohort to participate in mediation during each visit. The implementation of group-oriented healthcare presents a significant opportunity to expedite interventions for tobacco usage and nicotine addiction. Further information regarding instruments and interventions for tobacco cessation can be accessed by visiting the website www.askandact.org.

Electronic Health Records

Electronic health records (EHRs) facilitate the assimilation of evidence-based recommendations into the practice workflow. The AAFP promotes the adoption of Electronic Health Records (EHRs) that encompass the following functionalities:

An arrangement designed to encourage clinicians or their respective training cohorts to collect information pertaining to tobacco and nicotine usage, exposure to secondhand cigarette smoke, present cessation inclinations, and previous attempts to quit.

The clinical decision support system assists healthcare professionals and their personnel in assessing tobacco use, promoting cessation, linking patients and their families to relevant resources, and educating them about the benefits of a smoke-free environment.

It is recommended by the AAFP that individuals assess and monitor their use of tobacco and nicotine during every encounter or opportunity. Evaluations regarding tobacco use can prove to be advantageous in procuring essential data for a range of high-quality investigative initiatives.

Telemedicine for Tobacco Cessation

Despite the availability of tobacco cessation interventions in healthcare facilities, the utilization of telehealth services can effectively expand accessibility, improve adherence to chronic care management, and offer healthcare professionals advanced approaches to dispensing evidence-based treatment, particularly for addressing tobacco dependence."

Telehealth employs telephonic or video-based medical interventions catered through a patient's primary healthcare team, and serves as a viable means to augment the services offered by state-run tobacco cessation helplines. According to research, telehealth initiatives for smoking cessation serve as an effective tool in the treatment of tobacco addiction. In comparison to in-person counseling, such initiatives have been found to yield similar rates of abstinence from smoking during weeks 9 to 12. Additionally, they result in greater patient satisfaction and better adherence to pharmacotherapy treatment as compared to quitline-style phone counseling. These findings highlight the potential of telehealth to facilitate the discontinuation of tobacco use.

Installment Payment Plan and Eligible Covered Services.

The reiterated implementation of clinical tobacco suspension guidelines stands out as one of the top three critical and cost-efficient preventive measures that can be furnished in a medical establishment."21 It is imperative that health plan coverage and proper remuneration be extended towards evidence-based physician services intended for the screening and management of tobacco usage, in compliance with the recommendations annexed to the U.S. Preventive Services Task Force (USPSTF).30

The American Academy of Family Physicians recommends that all those who engage in tobacco consumption within the United States be cognizant of the availability and utilization of evidence-based, FDA-endorsed therapies and counseling. The remuneration of physician services associated with smoking cessation counseling provided to Medicare beneficiaries is borne by the Centers for

Medicare and Medicaid Services (CMS). As per the Patient Protection and Affordable Care Act (ACA), healthcare plans are mandated to extend coverage for a range of clinical preventative services that encompass tobacco use screening and counseling. Pertinent guidance on coding for tobacco cessation and screening is at the disposal of interested parties through the website of the AAFP.

High-risk Populations

Despite the overall decline in tobacco consumption, specific demographics continue to maintain elevated levels. Elevated rates of tobacco and nicotine usage within these communities substantially augment their susceptibility to deleterious health consequences. Individuals who are obliged to use tobacco include the following:

Individuals belonging to certain marginalized racial and ethnic demographics...

Individuals who identify as lesbian, gay, bisexual, transgender, or with other non-heteronormative sexualities and gender identities (LGBT).

Individuals with limited educational backgrounds and lower socioeconomic status.

Individuals residing in rural regions

Individuals that are afflicted with a mental illness.

Individuals who are experiencing substance misuse disorders.

Individuals with psychological maladaptation exhibit smoking rates that are twice as high as those observed in the general population. It is estimated that almost half of all cigarettes sold in the United States are consumed by people diagnosed with mental illnesses, with a notably high prevalence among patients with schizophrenia, bipolar disorder, depression, post-traumatic stress disorder (PTSD), and alcohol or substance use disorders. Additionally, the prevalence of smoking tends to increase as the number of co-occurring mental disorders rises, with approximately 61% of individuals diagnosed with at least three conditions reporting tobacco use.

Various populations having increased health hazards due to the usage of tobacco comprise of individuals who are expecting a child, individuals attempting to manage human immunodeficiency virus (HIV), and individuals who possess coexisting health conditions such as diabetes, cancer, cardiovascular disease, chronic obstructive pulmonary disease (COPD), diabetes, and asthma.

The Prevalence of Tobacco Consumption among Juvenile Population

In 2017, a staggering 3.6 million students attending middle and high schools were identified as regular tobacco consumers. Of this number, 7.6% of high school students reported smoking within the preceding month, with one in every five admissions indicating the use of various tobacco products. Despite the grave and enduring detrimental effects of smoking on health, adolescents are also vulnerable to immediate adverse impacts affecting their brain, respiratory, cardiovascular, gastrointestinal, immune, and metabolic functions.

Whilst the prevalence of youth cigarette smoking has decreased, the Food and Drug Administration (FDA) has reported a significant increase of 77% in the use of Electronic Nicotine Delivery Systems (ENDS) among high school students within a one-year period in 2018. This alarming trend has been identified as an epidemic by the Surgeon General's Advisory on E-cigarette Use Among Youth, released in 2018. Furthermore, the leading health advocate has firmly urged for decisive measures to tackle the rapid escalation of ENDS usage among young individuals, whose unfortunate resultant is nicotine addiction. The manifestation of nicotine use among young individuals may have detrimental effects on their mental well-being, thereby impeding their cognitive abilities including learning, retaining and processing information, as well as critical decision-making. The evidence also suggests that the utilization of electronic nicotine delivery system (ENDS) during the stage of pre-adulthood could potentially lead to the adoption of conventional smoking in the later stages of life. (Source cited as 44).

It is evident that there exists a clear and incontrovertible link between tobacco advertising and its effect on the initiation, prevalence, and inclination towards tobacco use among adolescent individuals. The promotion of tobacco products is extensively targeted towards younger populations such as teenagers and young adults. A report by R.J. Reynolds in the year 1984 illustrates the significance of these young adult smokers through their statement, "Younger adult smokers are the primary source of replacement smokers..." In the event that younger adults were to abstain from smoking, the tobacco industry's revenue is expected to diminish, much akin to a declining birth rate. The tobacco industry has exerted considerable effort and invested substantially to retain these consumers.

In the year 2016, the advertising and promotional expenses of cigarette and smokeless tobacco associations in the United States amounted to a combined total of $9.5 billion, as evidenced by reports 46 and 47.

The significance of tobacco avoidance programs is increasing as they serve as a crucial measure to thwart the initiation of tobacco use among young individuals, particularly as the tobacco and nicotine industry alters and adapts to appeal to novel demographics. Almost all adults who smoke regularly began smoking at the age of 26 or younger, with the majority (88%) initiating this habit prior to attaining legal adulthood at 18 years old. Despite some recent promising reductions in overall adolescent ENDS consumption, the usage of ENDS by middle and high school students remains alarmingly high.

Is It Advisable To Obtain Medical Assistance?

It is advisable that you engage in a consultation with your physician to determine the specific measures that can be undertaken to assist you in cessation. In the event of being a moderate or occasional smoker, it is plausible for your physician to proffer prescription medication that has demonstrated efficacy. Individuals suffering from asthma may benefit from the free nicotine replacement therapy provided by several pharmacies. This therapy has been scientifically proven to be safe and effective and can assist in smoking cessation.

Several states and local communities have established "Smoking Cessation Hotlines", which offer complimentary support and guidance to individuals seeking assistance to quit smoking. These are generally free, with no obligation, and usually offer free follow-up support. Each of these helplines provides current and comprehensive resources on smoking cessation, along with a range of aid and assistance to facilitate the process of quitting smoking.

If your physician proves ineffective in aiding you towards smoking cessation, you may consider seeking support from T-CAP, a government-funded initiative dedicated to facilitating smokers in their efforts to quit or prepare for quitting. This initiative offers complimentary assistance for cessation and gratuitous amenities such as pharmaceutical solutions, guidance on cessation procedures, and post-cessation sustenance. This program is intended for individuals who indulge in smoking habits at moderate to high levels and are resolved to quit.

For patients suffering from asthma, it is crucial to enroll in a smoking cessation program at the state or local level. Obtaining current, officially sanctioned recommendations for cessation of smoking is of utmost significance. It is advisable to consult with your physician who can provide a referral to a program of such nature. Furthermore, he/she can assist you in identifying and choosing smoking cessation medications that are compatible with your health condition. They may have some suggestions based on the treatment that has been prescribed to you on earlier occasions.

May I inquire as to whether I am able to utilize hypnosis?

Research has demonstrated that hypnotherapy is a viable technique in facilitating smoking cessation among individuals. According to research, hypnosis can be considered as an adjunctive intervention when used alongside other cessation techniques such as nicotine replacement therapy or medication, thereby enhancing the cessation outcome up to 25%.

There exist several distinct methodologies by which hypnosis can aid an individual in quitting smoking. An effective method involves the smoker listening to a hypnosis recording during sleep. This will facilitate relaxation and aid in directing their attention towards quitting. An alternative approach would involve seeking the aid of a professional hypnotist who can facilitate the smoker's journey towards becoming smoke-free through in-person sessions.

Irrespective of the modality employed, hypnosis facilitates the establishment of a conscious connection between smokers and their underlying motives for cessation of smoking while rendering them equipped with effective coping strategies to combat the allure of smoking. It further aids in mitigating stress and anxiety, prevailing after ceasing tobacco consumption, which are prevalent concomitants of tobacco cessation.

There exist numerous alleged advantages to abstaining from smoking by means of hypnotherapy. Nevertheless, it is imperative to weigh the pros and cons of implementing this approach before arriving at a conclusion.

The primary drawback associated with utilizing hypnosis as a means of smoking cessation is its potential ineffectiveness for certain individuals. Certain individuals have reported success in their endeavors to cease smoking through the utilization of hypnosis, while others have found such an approach to be ineffective in altering their behavior. Moreover, in case individuals are not able to quit smoking efficaciously via hypnosis, they might perceive it as a personal failure, which could further reduce their inclination towards attempting again.

An additional plausible drawback of using hypnosis as a method to cease smoking is the financial investment required. Although complimentary consultations may be available with certain hypnotists, the majority of hypnotherapy sessions involve a fee. Over time, the cumulative cost may become a barrier for individuals seeking to quit smoking.

Ultimately, it is worth considering that a potential drawback of utilizing hypnosis as a cessation strategy for smoking is that the resultant effects may manifest over an extended period of time. Individuals who receive hypnotic therapy frequently express experiencing an improvement in their symptoms following a few sessions. Nevertheless, those who seek to cease smoking must fully dedicate themselves to the treatment in order to derive maximum benefit.

Secondly, the practice of hypnosis can be rather costly. The fees for an appointment with a certified hypnotist can range from $75 to $200 per session.

In addition, it is noteworthy that the practice of hypnotism demands a substantial investment of time, with a typical duration of one hour per session for a minimum of six sessions.

Furthermore, an important aspect to consider is that certain individuals who have resorted to hypnosis as a smoking cessation aid have disclosed post-cessation episodes of cravings and urge to smoke.

Establishing a System of Positive Reinforcement

Individuals attempting to cease smoking frequently encounter a challenging predicament. They exhibit a strong passion to cease smoking, albeit being devoid of favorable resources or assistance. The implementation of a positive reinforcement system can facilitate your adherence to the smoking cessation regimen, ultimately leading to long-term success in quitting.

Individuals who are attempting to cease smoking often encounter a challenging circumstance. Perhaps you are encountering cravings and withdrawal manifestations that may challenge your commitment to abstain from smoking. A positive reinforcement scheme entails the dispensation of benefits for bespoke actions or conduct, such as the cessation of smoking. Compensation may encompass a spectrum of incentives, ranging from commendation through verbal accolades to modest offerings or advantages. It is imperative to select incentives that hold significance for the smoker and act as a driving force for them to strive towards their goal.

It is imperative that individuals establish pragmatic objectives as a component of the affirmative reinforcement mechanism. Ceasing smoking altogether may not be an immediately attainable objective for all individuals, hence individuals should strive towards accomplishing smaller goals like gradually diminishing their daily or weekly cigarette consumption by a certain amount. Incentivizing oneself upon accomplishing these incremental objectives can effectively sustain one's motivation throughout the process.

When establishing a system of positive reinforcement, it is important to bear in mind certain considerations:

Ensure to offer motivation and assistance throughout the course of action.

It is advisable to refrain from using negative language or resorting to punitive measures, such as stating that privileges will be revoked if the habit of smoking is not terminated.

It is important to maintain a record of the progress made and commemorate achievements at regular intervals.

Ensure that the incentives offered possess significant value and can serve as potent sources of motivation.

- Keep the system simple and easy to understand.

Ensure uniformity in the allocation of rewards.

Encourage the participants to commemorate their achievements throughout the process.

The implementation of a positive reinforcement system has the potential to serve as a valuable mechanism in facilitating smoking cessation among individuals. Offering substantial incentives for abstaining from smoking can foster an atmosphere of support which cultivates triumph.

Utilizing the Technique of Counting One's Breaths Upon Experiencing the Urge

The habit of smoking is an addiction that a substantial proportion of the populace encounters considerable difficulties in overcoming. When experiencing the desire to smoke, resorting to the technique of breath counting can prove to be helpful. Breath counting entails the systematic counting of each inhalation and exhalation, effectively quelling the urge to smoke. This methodology is applicable in situations where an individual experiences stress or an inclination to smoke.

The utilization of a breath counting technique could potentially assist in the discipline of one's smoking habit. The practice of counting one's breaths holds significant value for individuals desiring to curtail their tobacco intake, whether it be through the reduction of cigarettes or other tobacco-based products such as cigars or pipes.

Breath counting takes practice. After gaining proficiency in the skills of breath count and sobriety maintenance, you may then redirect your focus onto mastering this particular methodology.

Breath counting entails the inhalation of air through the nasal cavity, followed by the exhalation thereof through the oral cavity. Every respiration is quantifiable. The quantity of inhalations and exhalations that one must take is referred to as the designated objective figure. Commence with taking a single breath per 3 to 5-minute time span, and subsequently modify the duration accordingly.

The practice of counting breaths is considered a valuable technique in the management of cravings. By exercising self-control over your impulses, there is a reduced likelihood of requiring to smoke. If one is already a smoker and experiencing difficulty in quitting, it may be reassuring to realize that succumbing to the urge to smoke is not a compulsory recourse.

When one experiences the sensation of urge.

The practice of counting one's breath can serve as a useful technique when one encounters a temptation to smoke or experiences an urge to indulge in smoking. You may experience the sensation of craving for smoking even prior to contemplating about it.

Prior to commencing the process of counting breaths, it may be advisable to establish a predetermined numerical goal for oneself. For instance, it is possible for one to determine that they will discontinue smoking once they have consumed two cigarettes. One possible way to rephrase this statement in a more formal tone could be: "Alternatively, you may opt to engage in the practice of counting until a cigarette is consumed, or simply keeping track of the amount of cigarettes consumed."

In the majority of instances, one can utilize their inhalation and exhalation patterns as a coping mechanism to successfully manage and overcome their urges. If one encounters difficulty in overcoming the urge to engage in a particular behavior, employing the technique of counting one's breaths may aid in achieving the desired result.

It is imperative for the sustenance of life that your body receives an adequate supply of oxygen.

When one engages in the act of inhalation, oxygen is introduced into the body. Upon exhalation, the process of expelling oxygen from one's body occurs. As long as one continues the act of inhalation, an adequate supply of oxygen will be facilitated into their body. Furthermore, it is noteworthy that you exhale oxygen as well. Failure to exhale and utilize one's breath as a coping mechanism during smoking cessation can lead to the occurrence of an oxygen deficiency in the body.

It is possible that one may assume a lack of urge to smoke due to the act of breathing. Nevertheless, it is impossible to anticipate the precise moment when you may experience the inclination to indulge in smoking.

To initiate the practice of breath counting, begin by inhaling deeply and subsequently exhaling completely. Inhale and assign the numerical value of "one," followed by exhaling and assigning the numerical value of "two."

Please proceed with counting incrementally until reaching the numerical value of ten, subsequently recommencing the counting sequence from the beginning digit. Continue with this procedure until the impulse to smoke diminishes or for a minimum of five minutes, whichever transpires foremost. In the event that the notion of smoking should manifest in one's cognizance during the counting process, it is recommended to disregard said notion and proceed with the focus on counting the breaths.

Cigarettes And Stress

There is a widely held belief among individuals that smoking cigarettes can alleviate their stress levels or enable them to cope with it. This is not possible. Their understanding of the matter may be misguided and require further insight.

Cigarettes merely mitigate a fraction of the stress attributable to their own consumption. In the absence of nicotine addiction, stress levels would remain unaffected. This phenomenon transpires due to the reduction in nicotine levels in one's bloodstream, which induces feelings of agitation and restlessness. It has been observed that the human brain develops a strong desire for nicotine, which, in turn, has been linked with heightened levels of stress. To mitigate the stress, it is suggested that you engage in smoking. For the sake of clarification, allow me to provide an uncommon yet comparable analogy.

What is the potential consequence of encircling a rubber band around one's digit? Imagine wrapping it tightly. Upon experiencing a sensation of heat and discomfort in your digit, a sense of discomfort and emotional strain begins to manifest. When the level of stress becomes unbearable, one may proceed to remove the elastics to experience the momentary relief of the re-establishment of blood flow to the fingertips, thereby alleviating the discomfort. The individual's stress levels have been restored to a baseline level, thereby returning their physiological state to a state of equilibrium. Although the example may possess unconventional attributes, it is imperative that we assess it in relation to the aforementioned circumstances.

Would you say that removing elastics from your finger reduces stress? It indeed does so, albeit emphasizing solely the pressure resulted from coiling it around the digit. If one does not appropriately utilize elastic by placing it around their finger, it is incapable of providing any stress-relieving benefits, can it not? The usage of elastics alone does not possess a calming effect. Are you able to discern any resemblances or parallels to the act of smoking? I trust that this will not lead to you perceiving me as being erratic, for discussing the subject of elastics in a publication about smoking. For the sake of clarity, allow me to provide further elaboration.

Initially, an individual develops a nicotine dependence. At that point, nicotine becomes necessary for the purpose of alleviating the stress that arose as a result of prior nicotine consumption. In the absence of your addiction, you would not experience distress and consequently, would not require it. Upon cessation of nicotine intake, tension begins to mount within the brain. You appear to be experiencing heightened levels of stress, which may be manifesting in irritability. After smoking a cigarette, one feels no adverse effects. The resemblance to elastic lies in the fact that not winding it around your finger would not alleviate the tension that it generates when taken off.

Upon closer analysis, it can be observed that cigarettes merely alleviate the stress that arises as a direct result of their consumption.

Do cigarettes provide any viable means of alleviating stress associated with work? Alternatively, the anxiety experienced while commuting on the congested expressway en route to the workplace. It is posited that cigarettes lack the ability to effectively displace or otherwise facilitate the movement of vehicles on one's behalf. It is beyond their capability to effectively intervene and cease the act of verbal aggression exhibited by your superior. Smoking tobacco products does not bear any potential to assist in funding your home loan. May I direct your attention towards the direction that I am pursuing? Tobacco products are incapable of mitigating any external stressors. Your smoking habit will not exempt you from encountering stress-inducing events, which are commonly faced by individuals irrespective of their smoking behavior.

It is anticipated that some may express dissent towards the veracity of the aforementioned statement. Smoking has shown to significantly enhance workplace productivity and provide a heightened sense of well-being while navigating a congested roadway. Indeed, you do experience stress, albeit specific to the decreasing levels of nicotine in your bloodstream. Smoking tobacco products can potentially provide limited assistance in that regard.

During stressful circumstances, the urge to smoke intensifies beyond the ordinary. You do, right? In the event of encountering discomfort, one may experience a compulsion to immediately consume a cigarette. As an illustration, in the event of being on the brink of driving off a bridge, the majority of individuals who smoke would promptly halt their vehicle and proceed to light a cigarette. That was indeed a narrow escape, we almost fell off the bridge. It is your belief that smoking a cigarette has a calming effect on you during high-stress situations. It does not. The experience of cigarette craving in such scenarios is intricately linked to the physiological processes taking place within the body.

In the presence of external stressors such as driving, occupational demands, or public speaking, the levels of adrenaline and cortisol in one's bloodstream will elevate. The aforementioned procedure expedites the depletion of nicotine concentration in your bloodstream, thereby stimulating an urge to consume another cigarette earlier than anticipated. Consequently, the impact of external stressors is manifested in the acceleration of one's heart rate, elevation of blood pressure, and expedited removal of nicotine from the system, surpassing the usual pace. One experiences the inclination to smoke during a situation of stress, not due to the cigarette aiding in mitigating the stress, but rather due to the rapid depletion of nicotine levels in one's system, which necessitates an immediate replenishment to satiate the addiction. On occasions, when you are in a relaxed state akin to that of a leisurely Sunday morning, your frequent tobacco consumption may taper down to once every few hours. However, when confronted with acute stressors, it is likely that your impulse to smoke will intensify and precipitate an increased frequency of smoking.

Undoubtedly, the cognitive process occurring within your mind eludes your conscious awareness, consequently leading you to associate cigarettes with a soothing impact. One begins to associate smoking with the experience of pleasure and the alleviation of stress. Each instance of indulging addiction yields its own unique pleasure, without question.

I am uncertain regarding the reliability of this information. Could you please provide additional evidence or corroborating sources to strengthen the basis of this assertion? Suppose for a moment that my prior assertions are fallacious, and that cigarettes indeed confer a host of magical benefits upon the user. To commence, the aforementioned assertions have been substantiated by scientific research. Significantly, I validated it on myself! Solely an individual who was or is inclined towards nicotine addiction can genuinely empathize with smokers. Having had the opportunity to experience both lifestyles, I can confidently assert that upon abstaining from smoking, an individual is bound to experience a greater sense of calm and relaxation. There is no comparison. My current state involves a significant reduction in stress levels in comparison to the time period when I used to engage in smoking. Countless former smokers can provide you with a similar recounting. This is not a theoretical instance commonly found in scientific literature. This is an authentic firsthand experience.

When individuals posit that nicotine has a calming effect on their psyche, I educate them on the fundamental nature of nicotine as a stimulant. It elicits an elevation in both heart rate and blood pressure. What is the mechanism by which a stimulant produces calming effects? Your perception of its calming effect is likely due to your addictive tendencies towards it. From a physiological perspective, rather than inducing a state of calmness, it should elicit a surge of energy within you. However, it is infrequently observed.

Let's recap. Cigarettes are not efficacious in mitigating external stressors. They are unable to do so as they lack the authority to influence external events. Regardless of the quantity of cigarettes individuals may consume, the underlying issue remains prevalent. In order to find the solution, you will need to explore alternative approaches. It is important to note that consuming cigarettes will not serve to ameliorate the situation and may in fact exacerbate it.

The gratification derived from smoking is a delusion created by the cerebral faculties. Absent this illusion, one would promptly perceive the unfavorable facets of smoking. There would be no justification for you to engage in smoking. One might experience a sense of regret over jeopardizing their life in such a manner. Consequently, it is imperative that you possess those narratives. You need to believe them too. My realization of the true essence of smoking occurred upon my resolute determination to abstain from it altogether. I surmised that there could be a potential discrepancy in my perspectives concerning smoking. The majority of individuals within my social circle abstain from smoking, yet exude contentment. I surmised that a narrative must be unfolding within my psyche, persuading me to adhere to the notion that indulgence in this world necessitates smoking. Why me? Why is it that individuals can derive happiness without resorting to the use of death sticks? Several acquaintances of mine renounced smoking, and over the years, evinced remarkable improvements in their physical appearance, emotional wellbeing, and overall fitness. Is it feasible to lead a quality life bereft of tobacco consumption? YES!

I deeply regret having smoked for a period of 20 years. I am compelled to express my desire to revert to a prior moment, however, it is beyond my ability to effectuate such a change, and the same applies to yourself as well. One may consider the cessation of smoking as a potential avenue towards regaining one's health. One may assert their control over their life and demonstrate to both themselves and those in their vicinity that they are not subject to an addiction.

Please make an effort to re-read the preceding chapters thoroughly and repeatedly, until you have gained a comprehensive understanding of the mechanisms underlying nicotine addiction. As long as you persist in the belief that smoking confers any type of benefit, you will likely devise additional rationalizations to justify maintaining the habit.

Quitting For Good

It appears that you have made a firm decision to cease smoking. Congratulations!

The majority of individuals who engage in tobacco consumption frequently experience intense cravings. However, it is within your capacity to control and suppress such impulses.

When experiencing the inclination to smoke, it is noteworthy to bear in mind that notwithstanding the intensity of the desire, it is anticipated to subside within 5-10 minutes, irrespective of the decision to engage in smoking, chewing on tobacco, or refraining from either. Every instance of resisting a craving shall bring you a step closer to permanent cessation.

Decision-making

Similar to any form of addiction, the act of voluntarily ceasing to smoke can be a challenging endeavor, particularly when attempting to do so without the presence of a support system. There exist numerous methodologies to abstain from smoking and an abundance of resources that can assist you in the process. It is advisable to consult with your healthcare practitioner regarding the utilization of nicotine replacement therapy as a possible approach to curbing cigarette addiction. Enrolling in smoking cessation programs significantly enhances the likelihood of achieving a successful outcome. The aforementioned programs are made available through healthcare facilities, public health agencies, communal institutes, and occupational venues. At present, it is likely that you are aware that smoking poses a deleterious effect on the respiratory system, elevating the incidence of bronchitis, emphysema, as well as lung cancer. Moreover, it is a well-established fact that exposure to light can lead to an increased susceptibility to various forms of cancer, along with ocular ailments such as cataracts and premature aging of the skin.

Allow us to discuss a set of constructive measures that could potentially assist you in successfully abstaining from the habit at hand. This is a commonly recounted narrative that is often shared among individuals who smoke. If one possesses the earnest desire to abstain from smoking and is resolute in their determination to do so, the inclination to smoke will gradually diminish. And it seems that smoking a cigarette is the only activity that occupies your mind. One may experience irritability and weight gain. Are you under the impression that cigarettes do not pose a risk to one's health? Subsequently, it happens imperceptibly that you resume smoking. The majority of individuals who smoke have attempted to quit on multiple occasions, yet have not achieved successful cessation. Despite previous unsuccessful attempts, it remains possible for one to effectively discontinue said habit. Lots of people have. You just need to find the technique that works for you. And now, I shall disclose the methodology to you.

The initial day without smoking may pose a considerable challenge. Fortunately, there exists a plethora of guidelines and tactics that may aid you in abstaining from the habit. By acquiring knowledge about the appropriate strategies for smoking cessation, as well as by familiarizing oneself with the physiological effects of quitting, one can ensure successful achievement of their objective to quit smoking.

Effective methods to abstain from tobacco consumption.

1. have a plan

According to the American Lung Association, making adequate preparations and assembling a set of tools for effective self-regulation during the initial period of one to ten days after smoking cessation can significantly aid in attaining the requisite disposition. It is anticipated that this will pose a significant challenge.

Schedule a medical consultation. Upon the occasion of your visit, kindly apprise your healthcare practitioner about your inclination to cease smoking and deliberate with them on the most apt variants of nicotine replacement therapy or non-nicotine interventions tailored to your needs. friend. Learn about nicotine addiction. The act of smoking is not merely a deleterious practice that can be terminated at one's own discretion. Nicotine is a substance known to elicit addictive responses within the human system by altering the normal biochemical processes within the brain. Deliberately schedule and organize your day of absence from work. To sustain the current momentum, it is advisable to limit the planning horizon to no more than a fortnight. Elect to determine the methodology by which you will discontinue smoking. An instance of this is where one may opt for the "cold turkey" technique or alternatively, adopt a gradual progression. Plan for cravings. Draft a roster of strategies or palliative endeavors that may be readily employed to assuage the yearning to smoke. Several illustrations may include taking a stroll, consuming a refreshing beverage, solving a word game, partaking in fruit consumption, or engaging in a conversation with a companion.

2. Patience

It is a common tendency to withdraw one's efforts and anticipate a recuperation within a period of a month. Whilst I appreciate your proposal greatly, regrettably it is not viable under the current circumstances.

Upon cessation of smoking, we successfully conquer the dependence on nicotine, encompassing both the physiological and psychological aspects.

The experience of withdrawal symptoms and relinquishing long-held habits, which have been ingrained in our psyche for a considerable period, if not the entirety of our mature existence. It is reasonable to anticipate that a considerable amount of time will be required to dismantle the prior connections that have bound us to smoking and supplant them with fresh, more salubrious practices.

It is important to bear in mind that the act of ceasing smoking is a gradual progression rather than an instantaneous happening.

Please take a seat, unwind, and perceive time as one of your greatest allies. The potency of the cigarette abstention increases proportionally with the duration elapsed between the last time you smoked. Please exercise forbearance towards yourself and the procedure.

3. Direct your attention towards the current moment.

The early stages of smoking cessation are complicated by the psychological challenges posed by nicotine withdrawal. We are constantly preoccupied with thoughts of smoking and consistently concerned about the potential of abstaining from cigarettes.

For individuals who are new to smoking, the concept of abstaining from lighting a cigarette indefinitely can be daunting. If these ideas are not diligently examined, they have the potential to precipitate a relapse in smoking behavior.

Should you find yourself in a state of unease regarding the prospect of a smoke-free future, may I suggest reflecting on the preceding day and withdrawing temporarily. Remaining in this environment calls for consistent application and tolerance, yet it is attainable and an exceptional approach to retaining authority over your smoking cessation regimen.

Subsequently, as your cogitations oscillate, intentionally disengage by channeling your focus to the present moment you are encountering. Your agency to effectuate change in your life exists in the present moment and shall endure perpetually. I may not have the ability to alter the events of yesterday or anticipate what transpires in the future, however, I do possess the power to regulate today.

4. Please maintain a positive outlook on your progress.

According to research, the average human being typically generates approximately 66,000 thoughts on a daily basis, with roughly 66% of those cognitions being characterized as pessimistic or unfavorable. It may not come as a surprise that a significant number of these negative thoughts are directed inward towards ourselves. At first glance, it is often the case that we tend to be excessively critical of ourselves.

The process of smoking cessation requires steadfastness, and maintaining a positive outlook can fortify one against the vicissitudes that arise in pursuit of this objective. There exist several efficacious techniques that can be incorporated into the Smoking Cessation Toolkit.

Procure affirmative affirmations and concise self-motivating phrases to sustain your abstinence from smoking, for instance, "I possess ample fortitude to vanquish nicotine" and "I prioritize wellness over tobacco usage".

Maintain a journal of thankfulness. Maintaining a gratitude journal aids in cultivating a habit of focusing on the affirmative aspects of life, while simultaneously relishing the advantages of journaling for mitigating stress.

Seek assistance imbued with humor. The exploration of outlets of amusement, including but not limited to comical recordings, entertaining television programs, and jovial companions, could aid in the alleviation of tension and the cultivation of optimistic contemplation.

Be thoughtful to yourself. Direct your attention towards constructive viewpoints that foster your well-being, eliminate those that do not, in particular, ruminating over circumstances beyond your control, such as the time spent indulging in smoking.

Focus on the positive changes at the center. View previous attempts to quit not as failures, but as opportunities to learn from as you strive to improve your daily life by ceasing tobacco use at present.

If you attest to the affirmative alterations in your life, subsequent action will ensue effortlessly.

Please enter the context or situation in which the phrase is used so that I can provide an appropriate response. Expect and acknowledge that. Smoking cessation is an inherently challenging undertaking, and regrettably, there appears to be no viable solution for it. During those occasional non-work days, endeavor to immerse yourself in a state of detachment. At day's end, refrain from fixating on the unfavorable aspects of your perspective's surroundings. Assuming all factors remain consistent, strive to perform at your utmost potential despite any negative cognitive or emotional states.

Reevaluate negative reasoning. It is advisable to take note of any pessimistic thoughts that may arise, such as "I am incapable of enduring this any longer" or "this task is exceedingly difficult," and make an effort to replace them with more affirmative affirmations like "I am making a daily effort" or "this may be challenging, but it is crucial for my well-being."

The initiation of an efficacious long-term discontinuance strategy primarily stems from our perspectives.

How Cognitive Reframing Works

5. Deal with Yourself

When one decides to cease smoking at an early stage, it becomes imperative to exercise greater caution to ensure that one's physiological necessities are suitably addressed. Managing your physical state, notably throughout the initial stages of cessation, can aid in mitigating the discomforts arising from nicotine withdrawal.

The following compendium of recommendations shall aid in your comfortable traversal of nicotine withdrawal:

Maintain a balanced and nutritious diet. Your body requires high-quality nourishment at present as it engages in the process of eliminating the toxins caused by cigarette consumption from your system.

Get more rest. It is highly probable that the symptoms of nicotine withdrawal will result in a state of fatigue lasting for a significant length of time, typically around two weeks. If by chance you have become fatigued, do not attempt to persevere. Rest more if possible. More often than not, you will awake the following day feeling completely rejuvenated, and in such instances, you will undoubtedly cultivate a deep sense of gratitude for being free from the habit of smoking.

Hydrate. Water serves as an exceptional means of inhibition. It helps you detox all the more rapidly and functions admirably as a hankering buster. By maintaining proper hydration, one can experience an overall improvement in their physical condition.

Work-out day to day. The said practice is advantageous for both somatic and psychological welfare, and constitutes a potent tactic for managing urges to indulge in smoking. Ambling is a low-impact cardiovascular activity that constitutes an excellent option for individuals leading sedentary lifestyles. It is imperative that you consult your primary healthcare provider prior to embarking on a new exercise regimen.

Take a day-to-day multivitamin. Smoking depletes our reservoirs of various nutrients and supplements. Therefore, it is advisable to provide yourself with the much-needed boost that a high-quality multi-nutrient supplement can offer during the initial period of smoking cessation. It could potentially aid in expediting the process of restoring your energy levels.

It is essential to bear in mind that although nicotine withdrawal may not be an entirely comfortable experience, it is a temporary phase of recovery that is crucial to overcome.

6. Stay away from Alcohol

The interrelation between liquor and tobacco persists, as studies demonstrate a marked tendency towards relapse in individuals afflicted with alcohol use disorder in cases involving heightened tobacco utilization.

Regardless of occasional alcohol consumption, exposing oneself to a group setting that induces early relapse into drinking during the recovery phase can pose a significant risk. Please endeavor to exercise patience and avoid hastening the process. New weaklings are delicate. The opportunity will come when you can have a beverage without it setting off the inclination to smoke, however, don't anticipate that that should be inside the principal month, or maybe even the initial not many months.

Our approaches to overcoming nicotine addiction may vary, and hence it is advisable to refrain from rigid assumptions regarding the duration of the recovery process. If all factors are held constant, focus on your present situation.

In the event that a forthcoming obligation involves alcohol and you harbor apprehensions about it, interpret this as an indication to exercise caution and prudence. Kindly contemplate postponement until such time when you feel more emotionally stable. Moreover, in the event that smoking is not feasible, devise a plan in advance for managing the event without engaging in smoking behavior.

It is not a misrepresentation that you are striving to preserve your well-being by quitting smoking, therefore, accord cessation the deliberation it deserves.

Ensure that your cessation program maintains a prominent position in your list of priorities for as long as it may be required. You should endeavor to engage in activities that enable you to maintain your state of sobriety."

7. Explore Strategies for Effective Stress Management

We have deliberated upon the crucial aspect of not neglecting our immediate physical and mental welfare whilst grappling with the perils of nicotine withdrawal. It should be duly noted that our domestic well-being also holds paramount importance in this regard. Undoubtedly, stress and outrage represent two of the most formidable challenges to smoking cessation programs, as they can undermine and hinder the progress of such initiatives unless they are thoroughly monitored and addressed.

Premature termination can elicit a significant sense of strain, which may become overwhelming particularly when compounded with the stresses of one's daily routine, should one allow it to transpire. Endeavor not to succumb to fatigue, and dedicate a portion of each day to easing stress through an activity that brings you pleasure.

Presented herein are a few relaxation techniques aimed at aiding you in effectively managing the stress associated with quitting smoking:

Scrub down. Engaging in a shower is a remarkable means of alleviating stress and distracting oneself from the ruminations of smoking. Light a couple of candles, utilize some scented shower salts and simply enjoy the moment.

Take an energetic walk. Lacing up your tennis shoes and embarking on a brisk walk outdoors (even if for a mere 15 minutes) can aid in mitigating feelings of restlessness and stress.

Attempt representation. Kindly take a few moments to close your eyes and visualize a place that brings about a sense of relaxation, whether it is a physical location or one that is imagined. Make yourself comfortable, inhale deeply, and proceed to the designated location when you sense the buildup of tension.

Whether indulging in solitary moments with a good book, enjoying a warm shower, or engaging in a personal hobby, perceive these activities as safeguarding your commitment to quit smoking, instead of viewing them as self-indulgence.

8. Request Help

According to the data, individuals who have a strong emotional support system are more likely to achieve long-term success in quitting smoking.

Notwithstanding the help, you could get from loved ones, consider adding internet-based help to your quit program.

9. Stay With It

Several reputable cessation programs have been forfeited in favor of the notion of indulging in smoking in moderation. Refrain from succumbing to this notion. The most optimal approach to regulate the monster is to abstain from introducing nicotine into one's physiological system. The longer one abstains from nicotine, the greater the likelihood of sustained abstinence from nicotine.

In the event that you opt to indulge in smoking for just one cigarette or on a solitary occasion, it is highly likely that you will relapse into smoking again. There is a possibility that you may inadvertently increase your smoking consumption.

Regarding the cessation of smoking, the notion of a singular cigarette having the ability to persist is unfounded. They travel in packs.

In the same vein, smoking relapse coincides with the inception of cessation progress in one's mentality. Should the unfavorable thoughts regarding smoking arise, and if they prove to persist, the opportune moment has arrived to reaffirm your resolve.

10. Keep Up Your Motivation

It is commendable that you have ceased smoking, as it is a wise decision for one's health. Most likely a few. Endeavor to remain rational despite the influence of temporal or physical distance. Sustain the state of your memory by delving into the justifications for frequent cessation. With the passage of time, their prominence may not diminish, but exercising caution could perhaps mitigate their perceived significance.

Cessation of smoking constitutes a journey or undertaking. If you approach each day with a methodical and focused mindset, you will discover that what started as a daunting task will eventually transform into an enjoyable challenge.

11. It is advisable to refrain from smoking habits that may act as triggers.

Triggers refer to various stimuli, such as persons, locations, objects, and situations, that elicit the urge to indulge in smoking. On the designated cessation day, endeavor to refrain from stimuli that may incite the urge to smoke. Allow me to provide you with some useful cues in order to successfully navigate and overcome typical smoking prompts:

Please dispose of your cigarettes, lighters, and ashtrays, if you have not done so already.

Avoid the consumption of caffeine as it has the potential to induce feelings of instability. Attempt to consume water, holding all other variables constant.

Invest energy with non-smokers.

Proceed to a location where smoking is strictly prohibited.

Ensure sufficient rest and adhere to proper dietary practices. Exhaustion can trigger the urge to smoke.

Altere sua prática cotidiana para evitar a exposição a estímulos associados ao tabagismo.

12. Attempt nicotine substitution treatment

Please gather details pertaining to nicotine replacement therapy. The choices include:

Nicotine solution formulated for nasal administration or inhalation

Nicotine transdermal patches, chewing gum, and capsules are available over-the-counter without the need of a prescription.

These quickly effective therapeutic interventions are commonly deemed safe when administered concurrently with extended-release nicotine patches or any of the non-nicotine prescription drugs intended for smoking cessation.

In recent times, there has been a significant surge in the attention given to electronic cigarettes (e-cigarettes) due to their potential as a viable alternative to traditional cigarette smoking. Despite this, electronic cigarettes have not demonstrated to be relatively safer or more efficient than nicotine replacement therapies in aiding individuals in their smoking cessation efforts.

13. Bite on it

Exert oral efforts to counteract the urge for tobacco consumption. It is recommended to chew on non-sugar-containing gum or consume hard candies. Alternatively, one may consider indulging in raw vegetables such as carrots, nuts, or sunflower seeds to satisfy their craving for a crunchy and palatable snack.

14. Kindly take necessary steps to recall the benefits.

Kindly document your reasons for quitting smoking and resisting tobacco cravings, without any reservation or hesitation, on paper or through verbal communication. These reasons could include:

Feeling significantly improved

Getting better

Protecting your loved ones from the detrimental effects of secondhand tobacco smoke.

Setting aside cash

It is important to note that attempting a strategy aimed at overcoming the urge to use tobacco is always preferable to doing nothing. Moreover, each instance of resisting tobacco cravings brings one closer to being free from tobacco.

Day 29

Exercise:

Engage in merriment for a duration of five minutes. Don't stop laughing. One may experience a sense of discomfort, peculiarity, or self-consciousness, however, it is unimportant as the recommended action is to simply engage in laughter. Endeavor to evoke amusement within oneself without the assistance of any external source of humor or jest. In the event of uncertainty regarding the initiation of laughter, it may be recommended to begin vocalizing the sounds commonly associated with amusement.

Kindly elucidate on the emotions that you encountered during this particular undertaking. Numerous individuals have conveyed a sense of embarrassment or awkwardness as a result of this exercise, albeit such reactions are constructive.

However, the majority of individuals have also expressed an alleviating and optimistic sensation once they have finished the task at hand.

Analogous to maintaining a cheerful demeanor, indulging in a hearty laughter session for 5 minutes can prove to be an excellent technique to ground oneself in the present moment. Upon further consideration, it can be agreed that a sense of humor is a vital component for a fulfilling existence. How unfortunate is the individual who lacks the capacity to find amusement in life's encounters? After all, life can be humorous, notwithstanding the unpleasant and dismal incidents.

Chuckles can serve as a mechanism to unwind, loosen up, liberate oneself, as well as attain a state of serenity, even in the face of one's flaws, challenging tendencies, and hurdles. When one indulges in hearty laughter, perhaps even to the point of weeping, they shed all former personal convictions and revel in the liberation from the smoking habit.

Numerous individuals aim to cease smoking by adopting a "formal" method of quitting. It is highly advantageous to maintain a sense of equilibrium by acknowledging the gravity of the pernicious impact of smoking on one's physical, mental, and spiritual well-being, while simultaneously deriving amusement from the irrationality of one's addiction.

Fifteen minutes of profound contemplation and attentive respiration. Recite the affirmation: "Existence is magnificent, amusing, and authentic."

Kindly share your experience utilizing the hashtag #30DaysLaugh.

Day 30

Exercise:

Kindly procure a sheet of paper that you can retain and proceed to inscribe all that you appreciate, without any specific hierarchy of significance.

After each item enumerated, kindly pen down the phrase "Thank you."

Individuals who do not express gratitude towards the blessings they receive from life tend to experience discontent and suffering. Moreover, misconceptions about the self tend to flourish in an environment dominated by negativity. An individual who is truly appreciative has the ability to relinquish any possession or attachment at any given time. Cultivating a grateful attitude on a daily basis will not only promote contentment but also foster a sense of well-being. Allow your robust state to express gratitude.

Have you ever come across an instance where an individual expressed a deep sense of gratitude towards cigarettes and acknowledged the benefits that they have provided to them? The absence of gratitude towards the impact of cigarettes on individuals' lives is indicative of smoking's perilous and unwelcome cultural convention. Nevertheless, some individuals have acquired an appreciation for the knowledge gained from their adverse encounters with the consumption of a lethal substance such as smoking. Express gratitude for your cognizance and appreciate every instant encountered on this magnificent cerulean sphere.

Notably, smoking cigarettes not only poses a threat to one's health due to its toxic nature but also hinders the development of a thankful mindset and spiritual essence. Given the singularity of our existence in the present, it is imperative to consistently prioritize a mindset of gratitude and emotional wellness. Devote your time to those who express gratitude, and engage in activities that foster a sense of appreciation in the present instant. Be thankful.

Conclusion

Perseverance is key to success, as multiple attempts may be required to achieve the desired outcome. This particular treasure has been reiterated for numerous centuries. This assertion held in elementary school remains even more valid in the realm of adult life. The prevailing belief among individuals is that failing to overcome a habit upon the first attempt is indicative of personal failure. This assertion is unfounded. It is common for individuals to make several attempts before successfully quitting, hence it is important not to be too hard on oneself if initial efforts do not yield desired outcomes. Perpetually assimilate wisdom from one's errors and employ that erudition in subsequent endeavours towards cessation. Examine thoroughly the sequence of actions preceding your relapse incident and deliberate upon all possible factors and circumstances that could have served as triggers or impetuses for the resumption of smoking. May I inquire whether there are any issues or challenges occurring within your household? Is it work? Initiate measures to address those issues.

It is important to note that the occasional act of smoking during your recovery period should not be considered as a relapse. Perceive it as a minor deviation, and resume adhering to your established regimen. Employ the error committed as a valuable learning opportunity and catalyst to propel oneself to greater efforts in subsequent endeavors.

The aforementioned five techniques expounded upon in the preceding chapters proffer a comprehensive and efficacious means of assuaging nicotine dependency for the majority of individuals. One should strive to always keep their objective top-of-mind throughout this process, and maintain a high level of motivation in order to achieve success. Kindly consider seeking the support of your loved ones while also regularly consulting with your physician throughout your journey. If you adhere to these prescribed steps efficaciously, you shall expeditiously be on the path to convalescence. Best wishes.

Section One: Individual Guidelines

1. Get motivated.

It would be imperative to possess a compelling, intrinsic motivation to cease smoking. Seldom do individuals, who impulsively attempt to relinquish a habit, attain permanent cessation.

Several factors of a personal nature that could be relevant for your situation could include:

Regarding your well-being:

Your physician has apprised you that your continued smoking habit may lead to medical complications or even mortality.

To ensure your overall health and wellness:

Although your physician has not yet advised you, you are conscious that smoking can lead to adverse health effects, and as a result, you have opted for a more wholesome way of living.

In consideration of the well-being of your offspring/partner:

to ensure that they are not subjected to the harmful effects of passive smoking.

Relatives:

If you have intentions of initiating a family, it is advisable to terminate smoking prior to conception for better health outcomes.

Children:

To exhibit exemplary conduct to your children or impressionable individuals under your guidance or supervision.

In order to economize.

Upon the request of a cherished individual.

2. Compose a detailed enumeration of your premises and retain it in your possession.

When beset by the urge to smoke and finding oneself in a state of potential vulnerability, the presence of a personal inventory of reasons for abstaining shall serve as a motivational force for continued perseverance.

3. Please determine the method you intend to employ.

Would you be opting for a gradual reduction or an abrupt cessation, commonly referred to as quitting cold turkey?

The matter remains unresolved regarding the comparative efficacy of immediate cessation and gradual reduction in achieving success in smoking cessation.

Allow us to contemplate these alternatives through the utilization of an analogy. The act of smoking may be analogously compared to that of engaging in a romantic partnership. When one comes to the realization that the relationship is detrimental to one's well-being, there are three courses of action available.

Persist with the detrimental relationship.

Cease the romantic involvement but maintain a cordial relationship while making occasional visits.

walk away from it and never go back

The choice is yours. I reiterate that the decision ultimately rests with you.

The effectiveness of a particular approach may vary from person to person and is contingent upon individual circumstances. Determine a course of action for cessation and steadfastly adhere to it.

4. Map your goals.

If one opts for a gradual reduction in their activities, it is imperative to evaluate their intentions truthfully, ensuring that such a decision is not intended to deceive others or intentionally postpone the task at hand. Adhere to your ultimate objective of abstaining from smoking by establishing a definitive target.

Methodically record a specific date on the calendar. Then, during the period from the initial decision to reduce smoking to the eventual cessation, designate a set number of cigarettes per day or a specific interval of hours between each cigarette.

This will facilitate enhanced focus and sustained motivation.

Simultaneously, it is recommended that you impose minor trials upon yourself, such as resisting the temptation to smoke a cigarette or enduring a few extra hours without indulging in the habit, amidst this period.

Electing to cease tobacco use incrementally can be likened to consuming an elephant.

What is the most effective method for an individual to consume the entirety of an elephant? Step-by-step approach.

5. Measure your victory.

In case of choosing a gradual approach towards quitting, one may employ their calendar to demarcate their aspirations, and in the event of opting for an immediate cessation, the same calendar shall serve as a tool to gauge one's triumph over smoking.

Indicate each day of accomplishment by filling it in with color or identifying it with a sticker. Although it may appear juvenile at present, envision the profound satisfaction that will ensue when you inspect your calendar in the near future and observe an orderly sequence of vividly-hued markings or embellishments.

6. Celebrate your victories.

Initially, each abstained hour from smoking will be regarded as a triumph. If an individual tends to possess a predilection towards visual inputs, they may consider embellishing their diary or day planner with hues or drawings of a smiling face, representing each hour that they were successful in accomplishing tasks. Upon each stroke of the clock, a new hour of triumph commences - let us partake in jubilation!

After the passage of time, the frequency of your celebrations will transition from an hourly basis to a daily, followed by weekly, and eventually monthly basis. It is imperative that you commemorate every milestone, no matter how distant they may be.

7. Reward yourself

It is recommended to acknowledge and incentivize oneself upon achieving specific milestones. By abstaining from purchasing cigarettes, you will now be able to economize.

Strategically position a jar in a convenient location, and allocate any funds that would have been designated for purchasing cigarette packs towards it, subsequently observing the gradual accumulation of wealth therein.

Avail yourself of this monetary sum to felicitate your own self by any means thy desire - for verily, thou hast merited it!

Herein, we present a few suggestions for the possible types of incentives that may be offered to oneself, contingent on the amount of savings amassed:

After successfully refraining from smoking for a day, treat yourself to a relaxing soak in a hot bubble bath or indulge in a meticulously prepared dinner as a token of accomplishment.

Following a duration of one week, it would be beneficial to indulge in a pampering session such as a manicure or plan a visit to your preferred local attraction.

Upon completion of one month's abstinence from smoking, individuals may consider indulging in activities such as dining out at a restaurant or embarking on an excursion to an amusement park.

After the lapse of a period of six months, it may be possible for you to indulge in a luxurious spa experience or a refined retreat at a picturesque locale.

8. Psychologically prepare yourself to cope with the symptoms that may arise from withdrawal.

We must be forthright and transparent regarding this matter. Your body has developed a dependence on nicotine. The act of gaining admission is, without a doubt, the primary stride towards convalescence. When the body ceases to receive its customary doses of nicotine, it may manifest withdrawal symptoms.

Do not fret, the manifestation of withdrawal symptoms indicates that your physiological system is undergoing a restorative process from nicotine dependency. The duration of withdrawal symptoms typically persists for a span of two to four weeks and can be moderately uncomfortable and disruptive in nature, albeit rarely severe.

By adequately preparing oneself for the anticipated onset of withdrawal symptoms, one can effectively equip oneself with the necessary tools to overcome them.

Presented below is a comprehensive enumeration of the frequently encountered symptoms that arise during the withdrawal phase:

Exhaustion or weariness

Heightened susceptibility to irritation or agitation.

The term "insomnia" refers to a persistent difficulty in falling or staying asleep, which can lead to a variety of physical and mental health issues if left untreated.

One alternative could be "major depressive disorder."

Vertigo.

tightness in the chest

Experiencing a mild or severe involuntary reflex action, resulting in expulsion of air from the lungs with a sudden sharp sound, generally caused due to an irritation or congestion in the respiratory system.

A sensation of dehydration in the throat.

Escalated hunger.

Gastrointestinal disorders.

Difficulty in maintaining focus.

9. Ensure that you are emotionally equipped to face the impending period.

Your pattern of reliance on a highly addictive chemical substance as a coping mechanism for the challenges of daily existence is evident. Nicotine has become an inherent component of your daily regimen and has even served as a means to induce relaxation and unwind at the culmination of your day.

Be cognizant of the emotional toll that is likely to accompany any restorative process and equip yourself accordingly.

During the journey towards emancipation from addiction, one may come across sentiments such as denial, anger, bargaining and depression.

10. Please be ready for an experience of nicotine-induced sensation.

During the process of pulmonary recuperation, residual tobacco odors are discharged and expelled into the bronchi. Upon cessation of smoking, an individual's olfactory senses are significantly enhanced, leading to an increased ability to detect the emanation of nicotine vapors. This becomes increasingly apparent during a state of repose, as none of the other faculties are operational while in slumber.

The olfactory stimulus has the potential to elicit a perception associated with smoking.

There is no cause for alarm, as what you are experiencing is a reassuring indication that your body is undergoing a process of self-recovery.

11. Avoid quitting during PMS.

Ladies may wish to consider the potential impact of their menstrual cycle while contemplating smoking cessation.

The manifestation of withdrawal symptoms attributed to nicotine cessation may exacerbate in conjunction with periods of hormonal-induced emotional distress.

12. Be positive.

While it may appear to be a trite assertion, individuals with a constructive outlook are unquestionably more prone to achieving success when compared to their counterparts who possess a doubtful mindset, and this is particularly valid for those who harbor a defeatist attitude."

Abstain from fixating on the drawbacks.

Maintain a positive demeanor and refrain from indulging in self-pity, even if various aspects of your being seem to encourage such thoughts.

Positive people who express positive emotions are more adept at overcoming challenges.

A positive perspective will enable you to perceive and prioritize your ultimate objective, rather than becoming consumed with immediate challenges.

The cultivation of optimistic thoughts and emotions can serve as an effective antidote to the stress that may be encountered throughout the phases of withdrawal. As an illustration, it can be strenuous to maintain negativity if your attention is concentrated on the favorable impacts of cessation on your physical and mental wellness.

13. Be kind to yourself.

Cessation of smoking may induce a form of traumatic experience.

Your physiology may not favorably respond to it. In all honesty it's not going to be the easiest thing you've ever done.

Avoid relentless self-criticism due to your cravings, and refrain from denigrating your attempts to combat the symptoms of withdrawal.

It is advisable not to compare your progress with that of an individual who has ceased or is in the course of ending their journey, as your personal journey is unique and distinct to you.

Have faith in your own abilities and motivate yourself, for in the end, you shall reap the greatest rewards from your successes.

14. Tough love.

Certain individuals lean towards a structured and methodical method of surmounting challenges.

If you happen to be experiencing this condition, it may be worth considering the use of an elastic band placed snugly around your wrist as a potential solution. When there is an urgent urge to smoke, one can utilize an elastic band by stretching and releasing it. It may cause temporary discomfort upon application, but it can serve as a diversionary tactic until the yearning subsides.

15. Look in the mirror.

It has been established through statistical evidence that cessation of smoking contributes to enhancement of one's physical appearance.

The impact of premature aging is mitigated as a result of the cessation of exposure to hazardous substances originating from tobacco smoke.

Individuals who refrain from smoking shall experience improved ocular brightness, stronger and healthier nails, as well as glossy and lustrous hair.

I appreciate the enhancements to your appearance.

Contemplate your reflection in the mirror and allow the radiance emanating from your eyes to inspire and propel you forward.

16. An isolated mistake does not constitute a definitive conclusion.

Permit me to expound upon this aspect with a supplementary comparison.

If by chance your mobile device slips from your grasp, you expeditiously retrieve it and thoroughly inspect it for any possible impairment. Upon close observation, one may note that the device has withstood the fall without sustaining any damage, or alternatively, there may be discernible imperfections such as a minor abrasion on the cover or a fracture on the display surface. Nevertheless, it remains functional.

Typically, one would refrain from deliberately discarding the phone and subsequently inflicting significant damage upon it, resulting in fragmentation.

Similar circumstances arise when one encounters a setback while endeavoring to abstain from smoking. Committing an error should not mark the culmination of your endeavors. A single misstep must not deter you from moving forward. While you may have faced a temporary setback, it does not imply a permanent defeat.

Please proceed from the point where you left off earlier. It would be ill-advised to disregard the significance of the days or weeks leading up to your lapse.

If you wish to modify the color of your calendar, kindly proceed to alter its shade. If you happen to be utilizing stickers, it is advisable to switch to an alternative shape.

Kindly refrain from commencing the daily/weekly tally from scratch.

In the hypothetical scenario wherein an individual experiences a lapse on the sixteenth day. Commence discussing your cessation dates as 16 incrementing by 1, 16 incrementing by 2, 16 incrementing by 3, and so forth.

Eventually the number of days since your blunder will outnumber the days before and you're a winner all the way!

17. Learn from your relapse.

If one is able to derive valuable lessons from their mistakes, then it cannot be considered as a defeat.

Reflect upon the circumstances that precipitated your mistake and endeavor to abstain from such scenarios for a period of time. Please adjust your plan of action accordingly.

18. Avoid stressful situations.

Indeed, I am aware that despite any obstacles, it is imperative to continue with the maintenance of daily existence. It is not feasible to completely shield oneself from potential hazards by over-protecting, restricting access to information or secluding oneself in a remote mountain cabin for six weeks.

Nevertheless, it is imperative that you possess a cognizance of the factors that trigger feelings of irritation and stress within you. It would be advisable to possess a thorough understanding of the factors that elicit adverse emotional responses.

If feasible, during the initial few weeks, endeavor to abstain from situations which are commonly perceived as being stressful.

As an illustration, refrain from arranging a visit to the dentist unless you are experiencing a pressing dental matter. Despite being in optimal cognitive state, even the most courageous individuals experience anxiety when anticipating a forthcoming visit to the dentist.

19. Multiplicity is important.

The greater the diversity of intervention strategies employed in aid of smoking cessation, the more effective the outcome is likely to be.

Refrain from adopting a dependency mindset.

Disperse your support mechanisms extensively to avoid transitioning reliance from nicotine to an alternative substance. Ensure that your endeavors towards overcoming addiction are supported by multiple pillars.

20. The utilization of diversion can be a highly effective strategy.

Employ a form of mental diversion upon experiencing cravings. The inclination to ignite one's cigarette is transitory and subsides within a duration of five minutes. A brief interlude of three to five minutes would suffice.

Irrespective of the perceived triviality of a potential diversion, any act that effectively alleviates a craving is a commendable course of action.

Engage in a brief cognitive break by reciting the alphabet forward and backward, harmonizing with the amplified melodies of the radio, performing a series of simple stretches to alleviate bodily tension, counting the squares on the floor, modifying the layout of your workspace, embarking on a leisurely stroll outdoors, donning alternative footwear, tending to your oral hygiene, hydrating yourself with a refreshing drink, exchanging messages with an acquaintance, or spending a few moments interacting with a furry companion, as the range of potential diversions is vast.

Essentially, engage in an activity that effectively diverts your attention from the desire until it dissipates, and remain assured that it will indeed diminish.

21. Conduct an online search for further details.

The world wide web hosts a myriad of webpages, blogsites and articles exclusively devoted to smoking cessation. The following pages are intended to provide motivation and aid in maintaining focus.

The accounts of individuals who have successfully conquered their nicotine addiction serve as an excellent source of inspiration in achieving long-term abstinence from smoking.

22. Scare tactics.

The internet can also be an exceptionally informative medium should one require motivation to adhere to their objectives. The literature outlining the deleterious effects of smoking and nicotine addiction on one's health ought to serve as a persuasive force. If one happens to come across a visual representation of the lungs of a deceased smoker, the experience may serve as a permanent cure for any lingering cravings for nicotine. Please excuse the use of the pun.

An Introduction To Your New Life Free From Tobacco Products.

Certainly, I am aware that smoking cessation can present considerable challenges for those who are accustomed to the habit. I have had prior experience and have successfully accomplished the task. Nevertheless, in the event that you are genuinely inclined to cease, you shall eventually succeed, and once the optimal moment materializes, you shall prevail. You will develop the determination and resolve necessary to proactively pursue opportunities. If there is a singular factor which hindered my progress

By persisting beyond the point at which I originally contemplated relinquishing, people pushing me. Challenge yourself to go beyond your limits, as this will be the ultimate opportunity to succeed.

The assistance of someone to motivate and guide you is currently imperative.

It is a widely known fact that smoking is detrimental to the health of all individuals.

Extensive research has substantiated the fact that the inhalation of secondhand smoke is significantly more detrimental to individual health than active smoking. Indulging in smoking not only harms your personal wellbeing but also poses a significant threat to the health of those in your vicinity. Which rational individual would intentionally and wilfully jeopardize the well-being of their beloved ones? Numerous individuals habitually engage in smoking for an extended period, thereby rendering it arduous for them to relinquish the habit. Nevertheless, assistance and optimism are available to you, particularly if your desire to cease the habit has persisted for an extended period.

Fundamental strategies for mitigating unhealthy lifestyle choices are as follows:

What are the underlying reasons behind the initiation of smoking behavior by individuals? Certain individuals initiate smoking due to the belief

It exudes an air of sophistication, leaving an indelible impression on their social circle. They perceive that it reflects maturity or sophistication. For the majority, it is merely a result of social influence exerted by peers.

Regrettably, a considerable number of individuals commence the habit of smoking at an early stage of their lives. Unfortunately, many

Individuals may develop bronchitis, respiratory ailments, neoplastic conditions, or pulmonary disorders. During our adolescence, we deemed it to be the most appropriate course of action as it was in accordance with the conduct of our peers. Peer pressure. It is possible that we have acquired the habit as a result of observing our parents or grandparents smoking. As a child of ten, I recollect accompanying my father to his television repair establishment situated in Silverdale, Newcastle-Under-Lyme, wherein we voyaged in his Morris 1000 (popularly known as Moggy 1000) van, the malodorous atmosphere of which was infused with the scent of stagnant cigarettes. He would partially lower the window of his vehicle whilst smoking and intentionally expel phlegm from his mouth through the opening onto the roadway. An unmistakable indication that he was progressing towards the cancer which ultimately led to his demise. Stupid sod!

The impact of smoking on one's health remains indeterminate, as the potential consequences of refraining from smoking are yet to be fully comprehended.

quit now. It is possible that you have developed malignant growths in both your oral cavity and respiratory system, which may result in respiratory distress, palpitations, and ambulation difficulties. There are numerous possibilities that may ensue should you choose to persist rather than surrender at this moment. Without a doubt, I affirm that 'now' is the appropriate course of action. Nevertheless, it remains a verity that there exists an opportune moment for all individuals. I refrain from coercing any individual in this concise ebook as I am exceedingly aware of the repercussions that arise from adopting such an approach. In my personal experience, this behavior has resulted in physical harm to myself, such as a black eye inflicted by my irate father who was willing to go to extreme lengths for his next cigarette. Any recognising these signs?

Paradoxically, some individuals engage in smoking over extended periods without experiencing any adverse effects.

them. Is there not always one? Rest assured, the majority of individuals do not fit into this category, as the proportion of those who do is comparatively minimal. If you catch my intended meaning. However, with the passage of time, this demographic experiences a realization of lethargy, fatigue, and heightened susceptibility to frequent colds. Consider the advantages of ceasing smoking, as by quitting the habit, you can alleviate concerns over malodorous odors permeating your household, vehicle, or attire.

You will not be required to empty, wash or bear the odor of the unsightly ashtrays in the morning. You shall not be subjected to any odors apart from those naturally present in the ambient air.

By refraining from further indulgence, you can initiate the healing process immediately. Your

The human physique exhibits remarkable proficiency in performing this activity given the appropriate circumstances. You shall possess the ability to ambulate or respire without the aid of supplemental oxygen. There exist numerous rationales to...

Cease the habit of smoking, and may you experience utmost well-being. There exist several factors that hinder individuals from quitting smoking, one of which is the apprehension that they might experience weight gain. I have heard all of the excuses. Despite popular misconception, the act of smoking during the aging process is more likely to produce weight gain rather than weight loss. To enhance one's personal life, it is imperative to undertake measures to safeguard one's overall health, such as ensuring weight maintenance and cessation of smoking. The measures being undertaken currently hold the potential to pave the path towards a future marked by robust wellness and a prosperous culmination. After having taken all relevant factors into consideration, naturally.

In the event that you encounter challenges in discontinuing the pattern, we strongly suggest that you acquaint yourself with the knowledge pertaining to the matter.

drugs inside cigarettes. If this is not enough to dissuade and deter you, please give thought to the potential consequences of your actions, including a future wherein you rely on life-sustaining measures such as artificial ventilation or supplemental oxygen.

Establish A Clear Smoke-Related Goal

To ensure mutual understanding, let's clarify our definitions of terms related to goals and habits before discussing them further.

A goal is the desired end result in life. Your purpose is connected through your approach. You desire the change to occur. Your aim is to quit smoking permanently.

A habit is crucial to this process. That is how the goal is executed on a daily basis.

Your actions on a daily basis determine your accomplishments in life more than your goals. We need to break down your end goal into small daily habits.

Smoking involves small habits, as evident from your one-day quit. Throughout the day, you choose whether or not to smoke in various moments. If you smoke two or three packs of cigarettes a day, you are not smoking for most of the time despite having a severe habit.

You are capable of not smoking for long periods during your day. To break your continuous first-thing-in-the-morning habit, we need to replace it with a new habit. You'll discover that when you have a habit chain, if you break the beginning of that chain, the rest of the process becomes surprisingly easy, and we can stack healthy habits throughout the day to build up and support that one effective habit.

Creating Daily Health Habits

Habits are the daily actions that help us achieve a personally significant goal, emphasizing the importance of it being personally resonant. We must locate the appropriate one. With the vision board on your wall and the process completed, you now know your personal goal. Short-term pleasure often triumphs over long-term reward, as we live day by day.

Small actions hold the power to link your reasons for wanting to improve your life. Imagine starting your day with small actions that lead to a chain reaction of positive benefits in your life. Consume a nutritious breakfast, converse pleasantly with your dear ones, then commence work by prioritizing crucial tasks. Throughout the day, you achieve habits that benefit your main objectives. You'd achieve greater satisfaction, productivity, and a clearer career path with my guarantee. You can achieve this by concentrating on minor actions that align with your significant objectives.

These habits are effortless. Most can be completed in five minutes or less. But with repetition, their impact compounds.

Employ the S.M.A.R.T. Goals approach.

This term may be familiar to you. Building goals through S.M.A.R.T. is a precise manner. George T. wrote it for the first time in November 1981 in Management Review. Doran. Let me explain the five letters of S.M.A.R.T.

S – Specific. You desire a clear and meaningful goal that is straightforward and practical. Goal of 'stop smoking' requires more specificity. People often fail to note down a specific number when attempting to lose weight, which is a mistake. Being vague increases the chance of giving up after a minor win.

A vague goal is problematic. We can set specific goals to end our habit, such as reducing our daily cigarette intake gradually from three packs to one pack, then from one pack to five cigarettes, until we reach zero cigarettes per day.

M – Measurable. A measurable goal must include a numerical value. If I lose three pounds out of ten, I have completed 30 percent of my weight loss goal. Count your daily cigarette intake and make that your starting point, even if quitting smoking is your ultimate aim. Your goal is now measurable.

We often express our desire to quit smoking, but after smoking just one cigarette, we feel like we failed. Our objectives are fragile, and our attempt to give up can break at any point. A measurable goal increases your chances of success.

Attainable or Achievable. This is an achievable aim for this cycle. Quitting smoking abruptly from three or five packs a day is not advisable. Our aim is to make a timeline that suits your needs. You may need to adjust your goals during the process. You estimated three months, but it will actually take five. Adapting, not quitting. Alternatively, you could find yourself ahead of schedule.

R - Appropriate or Rational. We desire a purpose that aligns with our underlying motivation. You are already there as this book focuses on a single type of goal, with every reason shared being directly linked to it. You're already in the relevant zone, I think.

T – Time-Sensitive. This part holds the highest significance for me. If your goal meets the criteria of being specific, measurable, and time-bound, it qualifies as S.M.A.R.T. Let me demonstrate the reasons why. My goal is to lose thirty pounds in thirty days, which enables measurement of success and tracks the number of pounds lost. Twenty-six pounds lost equals six-sevenths of my goal achieved. That's pretty good!

Here are some S.M.A.R.T. goals for smoking. Here's more examples to help you achieve your first smart goal.

Stop smoking in three months.

Transition to vaping 50 percent in 30 days.

Convert entirely to vaping in two months.

Switch from red to white lights for Christmas.

Reduce cigarette expenses by $100 per month.

Let's implement diverse approaches to achieve measurable objectives. You can also stack goals just like habit-stacking. After reaching one goal, strive for the next. You may need to use other techniques like group support or vaping to help yourself.

Quit smoking with a tool, then quit the tool itself. Switching from smoking to vaping allows you to eventually quit vaping altogether.

Shall we take complete control now?

Reflection Questions

Failed past goals?

Why set flexible objectives?

Are you playing it safe from the start?

Will elaborating on S.M.A.R.T. goals increase success?

Are you scared of setting S.M.A.R.T. goals and not achieving them?

Are you willing to stay with me on this journey and fight for the life you deserve?

Your Action Plan

Secure your definitive objective at present. What are your long-term goals and timeline? Put into practice all that is covered in this chapter. Record your responses in your notebook, then push further. Divide your goal into smaller parts.

Write down a decreasing number of daily cigarette allowance on a calendar for 30 days to quit smoking 30 cigarettes per day.

Record your end objective on your calendar for daily progress monitoring. I urge you to share it with others in a community or on Facebook for our support, motivation, and accountability to ensure you achieve your goal.

www.ingramcontent.com/pod-product-compliance
Lightning Source LLC
Chambersburg PA
CBHW071125130526
44590CB00056B/2041